FROM DEBT TO WEALTH

ALDO LAURAMZ

FROM DEBT TO WEALTH

The Ultimate Guide to Achieving Financial Independence

ISBN: 978-0-9996024-9-2

From Debt to Wealth:
“The Ultimate Guide to Achieving Financial Independence"

warranties of merchantability or fitness for a particular purpose.

CONTENTS

Each chapter provides practical information and tools, as well as real-life examples and stories that will help readers apply the advice to their own financial lives.

INTRODUCTION

The economy can be a source of stress and anxiety for many people, especially when facing a financial crisis.

Whether you are struggling to pay off debts, find a job or start a successful business, or simply manage your money effectively, it can be difficult to know where to begin. But don't worry, you're not alone. In "From Debt to Wealth", you will find practical advice, tools, and strategies to overcome your financial challenges and build a solid and successful financial life.

Through this book, you will learn how to get out of debt, manage your money effectively, find employment or start a successful business, set realistic and achievable financial goals, and more. Additionally, you will be inspired by real stories of people who have overcome their financial crises and achieved success.

But this book is not just a practical guide, it's also an invitation to change your mindset and develop a positive and proactive attitude towards your finances.

You will discover how to face your fears, overcome your limitations, and pursue your financial dreams with confidence and determination.

This book is not intended to offer quick and easy solutions, but to provide you with the tools and motivation you need to build a prosperous and sustainable financial life. So, if you're ready to take the first step towards financial freedom, let's embark on this journey together! Throughout this book, I will provide you with practical tools and valuable advice to help you get out of debt, manage your money effectively, find employment or start a successful business, set realistic and achievable financial goals, and much more.

Through this guide, you will discover how to develop a positive and proactive attitude towards your finances and how to learn from your mistakes and failures.

In addition, you will find real stories of people who have overcome their own financial challenges and have achieved financial success.

You will learn from their experience and motivation and find encouragement and guidance to face your own financial challenges. Remember that building a healthy and prosperous financial life doesn't happen overnight, but requires time, effort, and commitment. But you're not alone on this journey.

This book is here to guide, support, and motivate you every step of the way. So, if you're ready to take control of your finances and build a solid and successful financial future, keep reading!

PREFACE

The economy can be a source of stress and anxiety for many people, especially when facing a financial crisis.

However, you don't have to let debts and financial problems overwhelm you. With the right knowledge and tools, you can overcome economic difficulties and take control of your financial situation.

This book is designed to help you do just that. Through its pages, you will find practical advice, tools, and strategies to get out of debt, manage your money effectively, find employment or start a successful business, set realistic and achievable financial goals, and more. Additionally, this book will not only provide you with information and tools, but also inspire you through real stories of people who have overcome their economic crises and achieved financial success.

You will learn from their experience and motivation and find encouragement and guidance to face your own financial challenges.

Remember that building a healthy and prosperous financial life doesn't happen overnight, but requires time, effort, and commitment.

But you're not alone on this journey. This book is here to guide, support, and motivate you every step of the way.

So, without further ado, I invite you to dive into these pages and start building a more solid and successful financial future for you and your family.

Part I
Getting Out of Debt

1

WHY IS IT IMPORTANT TO GET OUT OF DEBT?

Getting out of debt is important for several reasons:

1. Financial freedom: Debts can limit your spending capacity and reduce your financial freedom. Being debt-free gives you more control over your money and allows you to spend it as you wish without worrying about monthly payments.
2. Reduced stress: Debts can be a major source of stress and anxiety. Getting out of debt can help reduce this emotional burden and improve your overall well-being.
3. Money savings: Being debt-free allows you to save more money in the long run, as you won't have to pay additional interest and charges.
4. Improved credit score: By getting out of debt and paying your bills on time, you can improve your credit score and become more attractive to lenders and credit providers in the future.

In summary, getting out of debt is important because it allows you to have more financial freedom, reduce stress and anxiety, save more money in the long run, and improve your credit score.

2

IDENTIFYING PRIORITY DEBTS

It is important to make a list of all debts and prioritize them according to their importance and urgency. Debts with high interest rates or those that are accumulating rapidly can be considered a priority.

Here is an example format for prioritizing your debts and keeping track of payments:

Debt Name	Current Balance	Interest Rate	Minimum Payment	Due Date	Priority
Credit Card A	$5,000	20%	$100	15th of each month	High
Personal Loan	$10,000	8%	$250	1st of each month	Medium
Car Loan	$15,000	4%	$350	5th of each month	Low
Medical Bill	$1,000	0%	$50	20th of each month	Low

In this format, debts are organized into a table with columns that include current balance, interest rate, minimum payment, due date, and priority.

The priority column is used to rank the debts as high, medium, or low priority. Debts with higher interest rates, such as credit cards, are classified as high priority, while debts with lower interest rates are classified as low priority.

To keep track of payments, it is important to record the payments made in the table, updating the current balance and due date of each debt. This will allow you to keep track of your payments and know how much you have left to pay on each debt.

Remember that this is just an example format and you can customize it according to your needs. The important thing is to keep a record of your debts and payments to prioritize your debts and avoid falling into default.

Establishing a Payment Plan: Once debts have been prioritized, a payment plan that suits the financial situation can be established. This may include minimum monthly payments or accelerated payments to reduce debt more quickly.

If debts are too large and cannot be paid effectively, it may be considered seeking professional help through a financial advisor or a credit counseling organization.

3

NEGOTIATING WITH CREDITORS

- Identify current financial situation: Before negotiating with creditors, it is important to have a clear understanding of the current financial situation and the ability to pay.
- Establish priorities: When negotiating with creditors, it is important to establish priorities and focus on debts that are more urgent or have more serious consequences.
- Contact creditors: It is important to contact creditors as soon as possible to discuss payment options and negotiate a payment plan.
- Be honest and transparent: When negotiating with creditors, it is important to be honest and transparent about the financial situation and ability to pay.
- Offer a realistic payment plan: It is important to present a realistic payment plan that is affordable and sustainable in the long term.
- Explore debt consolidation options: In some cases, consolidating debts into a single payment may be an option to reduce debt burden and make payment easier.
- Consider professional financial counseling: If you feel overwhelmed or unsure how to negotiate with creditors, seeking professional financial counseling may be helpful.

- Regular follow-up: Once a payment plan has been established, it is important to regularly follow up with creditors to ensure the plan is being met and make adjustments if necessary.

When negotiating with creditors, payment agreements can be sought that include interest reductions or elimination of late payment fees. It is important to be honest about the financial situation and maintain open and respectful communication with creditors.

Here is a model letter for negotiating with creditors:

[Your Name]
[Your Address]
[City, State ZIP Code]
[Date]

[Creditor's Name]
[Creditor's Address]
[City, State ZIP Code]

Dear [Creditor's Name],

I am writing to discuss the debt I owe to your company. I am committed to resolving this debt and I would like to work with you to find a mutually agreeable solution.

I understand that I am currently delinquent on my payments and I take full responsibility for this. However, due to [explain the reason for your financial difficulties such as job loss, medical expenses, etc.], I have been unable to meet my financial obligations.

I am currently working on a plan to catch up on my payments and would like to explore the possibility of establishing a payment plan that is both affordable and sustainable in the long term. I am also willing to consider other options that may be viable for both parties.

I would appreciate it if we could discuss this situation together and find a solution that works for both of us. Please feel free to contact me to discuss any proposals you may have.

Thank you for your attention to this matter.

Sincerely,

[Your Name]

Remember to personalize the letter according to your specific situation and the needs of your negotiation. It is important to be honest and present a realistic and fair proposal for both parties.

Avoiding new debts: Once the debt has been reduced, it is important to maintain a responsible attitude and not fall into the same financial traps.

This may include establishing healthy spending and saving habits, creating an emergency fund, and carefully planning credit purchases.

Here is an example of a format for creating an emergency fund:

Expense Category	Monthly Amount	Target Emergency Fund Amount
Housing	$1,200	$3,600
Utilities	$200	$600
Food	$400	$1,200
Transportation	$300	$900
Insurance	$150	$450
Health Care	$100	$300
Other Expenses	$250	$750
Total	$2,600	$7,800

In this example, the chart includes various expense categories and their corresponding monthly amounts. The target emergency fund amount is calculated by multiplying the monthly amount by three, which represents three months' worth of expenses.

To use this chart, first calculate your monthly expenses for each category and fill in the "Monthly Amount" column. Then, multiply each monthly amount by three and fill in the "Target Emergency Fund Amount" column. Finally, add up all of the target emergency fund amounts to determine your total emergency fund goal.

Remember that this is just an example format and you should adjust it based on your own expenses and emergency fund goals. The important thing is to have a clear understanding of your monthly expenses and a specific target emergency fund amount to work towards.

To analyze and understand how the debt was generated:

Identifying the underlying causes of the debt (unnecessary expenses, lack of income, etc.) can help create healthier financial habits in the long term.

Establishing a payment plan focused on the interest rate: It is recommended to establish a payment plan that focuses the maximum possible financial resources on the debt with the highest interest rate. This will help reduce the total amount of interest paid and accelerate the payment process.

Making sacrifices in the short term: Sometimes, it may be necessary to make sacrifices in the short term, such as reducing entertainment expenses or giving up certain luxuries, to reduce debt in the long term.

Seeking the advice of a financial expert: Seeking the advice of a financial expert is beneficial to create a payment plan that suits personal financial situations. A financial advisor can also help identify opportunities to consolidate debts or renegotiate interest rates.

4

ESTABLISHING A PAYMENT PLAN

- Evaluate financial situation: Before establishing a payment plan, it's important to evaluate the current financial situation, including the total amount of debt and available income.
- Prioritize debts: It's important to prioritize debts and focus on those with higher interest rates or late fees.
- Create a detailed budget: Creating a detailed budget can help identify areas where expenses can be reduced, and income increased to allocate more funds towards debt repayment.
- Establish financial goals: Setting realistic and achievable financial goals can help maintain focus and motivation while paying off debts.
- Establish a payment plan: Once prioritized debts have been identified and a detailed budget created, a payment plan can be established. This may include determining the amount of monthly payments, due dates, and payment methods.
- Consider debt consolidation: In some cases, consolidating debts into a single payment may be an option to reduce the burden of debt and make repayment easier.

- Regularly follow up: It's important to regularly follow up with creditors to ensure the payment plan is being met and make adjustments if necessary.
- Celebrate achievements: When establishing a payment plan and making regular payments, it's important to celebrate achievements and maintain a positive attitude towards the financial situation.

Here's an example of a payment plan format:

Debt Type	Current Balance	Minimum Payment	Agreed Payment	Start Date	End Date	Amount Paid
Credit Card A	$5,000	$100	$150	01/01/2023	06/30/2024	$1,000
Credit Card B	$3,000	$75	$100	01/01/2023	12/31/2023	$500
Personal Loan	$8,000	$200	$250	01/01/2023	12/31/2024	$1,500
Total	$16,000	$375	$500	-	-	$3,000

In this format, the different debts included in the payment plan are listed, along with their current balance, minimum payment, and the agreed payment amount. The start and end dates of the payment plan are also included, as well as the amount paid to date.

It's important to note that this is just an example format and can be customized to fit your specific needs. The key is to create a realistic payment plan that prioritizes debts with high-interest rates or penalties, sets achievable goals, and includes regular follow-ups to ensure the plan is on track.

5

AVOIDING NEW DEBTS

1. Evaluate spending habits: It's important to evaluate spending habits and be aware of unnecessary expenses that can lead to new debts.
2. Create a detailed budget: Creating a detailed budget can help identify areas where expenses can be reduced, and incomes can be increased to avoid new debts.
3. Set financial priorities: Setting clear financial priorities and focusing on achieving long-term financial goals can help avoid unnecessary expenses and new debts.
4. Avoid impulsive spending: Avoiding impulsive spending and taking time to evaluate significant purchases can help avoid new debts.
5. Avoid quick loans and high-interest credit cards: Avoiding quick loans and high-interest credit cards can reduce the temptation to incur new debts.
6. Establish an emergency fund: Establishing an emergency fund can help cover unexpected expenses without having to resort to new debts.
7. Consider additional income options: Considering options to generate additional income, such as part-time jobs or online sales, can help avoid new debts.

8. Seek financial advice: If you feel overwhelmed or unsure of how to avoid new debts, seeking professional financial advice can be helpful.

6

REGULAR MONITORING OF PROGRESS AND CREDIT SCORE

To regularly monitor your progress and credit score, you can follow these steps:

1. Request a free credit report: You can request a free credit report from credit agencies once a year. It's important to review your credit report to ensure there are no errors or fraud that may affect your credit score.
2. Subscribe to a credit monitoring service: There are credit monitoring services that allow you to regularly check your credit score and receive alerts in case of significant changes in your credit report.
3. Use expense tracking apps: Expense tracking apps allow you to monitor your expenses and ensure you're sticking to your budget.
4. Review your monthly statements: It's important to review your monthly statements to ensure there are no incorrect or unexpected charges.
5. Update your personal and financial information: If there are changes in your personal or financial information, such as a change of address or a salary increase, it's important to update this information in your credit report and with your lenders.

By regularly monitoring your progress and credit score, you can quickly detect problems and take steps to address them. This will allow you to maintain good financial health and work towards your long-term financial goals.

Part II
Effective Money Management

7

ESTABLISHING A REALISTIC BUDGET

Establishing a budget is an important part of any financial plan. Here are some steps you can follow to establish a budget:

1. Calculate your income: Identify all of your monthly income, including wages, business income, interest, dividends, and any other income you have.
2. Track your expenses: Determine your monthly expenses, including fixed expenses such as rent, utilities, loan payments, and variable expenses such as food, entertainment, and shopping.
3. Identify areas to cut expenses: Look for ways to reduce your expenses. This could include limiting impulsive purchases, eating at home instead of eating out, canceling subscriptions you don't use, etc.
4. Allocate an amount for savings: Allocate a monthly amount for savings. This may include an emergency fund, retirement savings, and any other long-term financial goal.
5. Prioritize your expenses: Identify your most important expenses and make sure they are covered first, such as rent, utilities, and loan payments. Then allocate the rest of your budget to other expenses.
6. Use tools to help stay on budget: There are many tools that can help you stay on budget, such as budgeting apps,

spreadsheets, etc. Use these tools to track your expenses and make sure you're sticking to your budget.

Remember, a budget is an important tool to help you control your spending and reach your financial goals. Be sure to review and adjust your budget regularly to make sure it's working for you.

Example of a Monthly Budget Format:

Income:

- Salary: $3,500
- Business Income: $500
- Interest: $50
- Total Income: $4,050

Expenses:

- Housing: $1,000 (rent, utilities, internet)
- Transportation: $300 (gas, vehicle maintenance, insurance)
- Food: $400 (groceries, eating out)
- Entertainment: $200 (movies, concerts, recreational activities)
- Clothing: $100
- Health and Personal Care: $150 (medical expenses, personal care products)
- Loan Payments: $500 (student loan, car loan)
- Savings: $350
- Total Expenses: $3,000

Balance:

- Total Income: $4,050
- Total Expenses: $3,000
- Remaining Balance: $1,050

In this example, the total monthly income is $4,050 and the total monthly expenses are $3,000, leaving a balance of $1,050 for savings or other expenses. Remember that this is just an example, and each budget should be customized based on individual needs and goals.

8

SAVING FOR EMERGENCIES

How to save for emergencies:

1. Identify your essential expenses: Determine which essential expenses you need to cover in case of an emergency, such as rent, utilities, medical expenses, and loan payments.
2. Determine your savings goal: Figure out how much money you need to save to cover these essential expenses. Experts recommend saving at least 3 to 6 months' worth of essential expenses.
3. Set a timeframe: Set a timeframe for achieving your savings goal. While saving that amount may seem daunting, setting a realistic timeframe can help you stay focused and motivated.
4. Establish a budget: Set a budget to ensure you are saving regularly and to identify areas where you can reduce expenses to contribute to your emergency fund.
5. Automate your savings: Set up an automatic transfer from your checking account to your savings account each month so that saving becomes an automatic task and you don't forget.
6. Look for secure investment options: Consider secure investment options such as high-yield savings accounts,

money market accounts, or certificates of deposit (CDs) so that your money is safe and earns interest while you save.

Remember that having an emergency fund can help you be prepared in case of a financial emergency. Be sure to review and adjust your savings plan regularly to ensure you are reaching your savings goal and are prepared for any emergency situations that may arise.

Example of Emergency Savings Format:

1. Identify your essential expenses:

- Rent: $1,000
- Utilities: $200
- Medical expenses: $100
- Loan payments: $300
- Total essential expenses: $1,600

2. Determine your savings goal:

- Save 6 months' worth of essential expenses
- Total savings goal: $9,600

3. Set a timeframe:

- Timeframe: 12 months
- Required monthly savings: $800

4. Establish a budget:

- Monthly income: $3,500
- Total monthly expenses: $2,500
- Budget available for savings: $1,000

5. Automate your savings:

   Set up an automatic transfer of $800 to a savings account each month.

6. Look for secure investment options:

   Open a high-yield savings account or consider investing in a short-term CD.

In this example, the person identifies their essential expenses and determines that they need to save $9,600 to cover six months' worth of those expenses. They set a 12-month timeframe to achieve their savings goal and establish a budget that allows them to save $1,000 each month. They then automate their savings and look for secure investment options. This format can be customized to suit each person's needs and goals.

9

INVESTING FOR THE FUTURE

Here are some steps you can follow to invest for the future:

1. Set financial goals: Setting clear and realistic financial goals can help you define your investment objectives and create a solid plan.
2. Know your investment profile: Before starting to invest, it is important to know your investment profile, which includes your risk tolerance, investment horizon, and financial goals. This will help you choose the appropriate investment strategy.
3. Diversify your portfolio: One way to minimize investment risks is to diversify your portfolio. This means investing in different types of assets, such as stocks, bonds, and real estate.
4. Research and analyze: Before making any investment, it is important to research and analyze the available investment options to make informed and prudent decisions.
5. Consult a professional: If you have no investment experience, consider consulting a financial professional to advise you and help you make smart investment decisions.
6. Keep your long-term goals in mind: Investing is a long-term process, so it is important to keep your long-term goals in

mind and be patient while waiting for your investments to mature.

Remember that investing can be an effective way to grow your wealth and secure your financial future, but it is always important to do so with caution and a solid plan in mind.

There are several investment options available for those looking to invest for the future. Some popular options include:

1. Stocks: Stocks are an investment in which you purchase a part of ownership in a company. If the company succeeds, the value of your stocks can increase and you can earn profits through dividends.
2. Bonds: Bonds are an investment in which you lend money to an entity, such as a government or a company, in exchange for interest. Bonds are often considered a safer investment than stocks.
3. Mutual funds: Mutual funds are an investment that combines the money of several investors to purchase a diversified portfolio of stocks, bonds, and other securities.
4. Real estate: Investing in real estate involves buying properties to rent or sell in the future. Real estate can be a solid long-term investment, but it requires a significant amount of initial capital.
5. Retirement savings: Retirement savings plans, such as 401(k) plans and IRA plans, are a popular way to invest for the future and ensure stable income during retirement.

Remember that before investing, it is important to research and analyze your investment options and know your investment profile to make informed and prudent decisions.

10

AVOIDING UNNECESSARY EXPENSES

To avoid unnecessary expenses, you can follow these tips:

1. Make a budget: It's important to have a budget to know exactly how much you're spending in each category, such as housing, food, transportation, among others. This way, you can identify unnecessary expenses and make adjustments to reduce them.
2. Buy only what you need: Before making a purchase, think if you really need the item or if it's just a whim. You can establish a shopping list and stick to it to avoid buying unnecessary things.
3. Compare prices: Before making a purchase, compare prices in different stores or online to find the best deal. This can help you save money on your purchases.
4. Avoid impulse purchases: Impulse purchases can lead you to spend money on things you don't need. Try to resist temptation and think if you really need the item before buying it.
5. Use coupons and offers: Use coupons and offers to save money on your purchases. You can find coupons online or in the newspaper, or take advantage of special offers in stores and restaurants.
6. Cancel unnecessary subscriptions: Review your monthly subscriptions, such as streaming services, magazines, or

gym memberships, and cancel those that you're not using or that are not essential.

7. Plan your purchases: Plan your purchases in advance to take advantage of the best deals and avoid impulse purchases. You can establish a budget for your Christmas shopping, for example, and buy gifts in advance.

Remember that avoiding unnecessary expenses is an important part of responsible financial management and can help you save money in the long term.

Selling everything you have in storage can be an option to get some extra money and free up space in your home or simply reduce an unnecessary expense such as storage rental. Here are some steps you can follow to sell the items in your storage:

- Review your items: Make an inventory of the items in your storage and decide which ones you want to sell. Make sure the items are in good condition and are valuable enough to sell.

- Set a fair price: Research market prices for similar items to determine a fair price for your items. Consider the condition, age, and brand of the items when setting the price.

- Choose a selling platform: There are many options available to sell your items, such as eBay, Amazon, Facebook Marketplace, MercadoLibre, among others. Choose the platform that best suits your needs and has an appropriate audience for your items.

- Take photos of the items: Take high-quality photos of the items you want to sell. Make sure the photos show important details and are well-lit.

- Create a detailed description: Create a detailed description of the items you're selling. Include details such as the brand, model, condition, and any other relevant information.
- Post your items for sale: Post your items on the platform you've chosen for sale. Make sure to include all the photos and detailed description you've created.
- Manage sales: Once your items are posted, manage the sales and communicate with buyers to agree on sale details, such as shipping or pickup.

Remember that selling the items in your storage can be a good option to get some extra money, but it's also important to consider if the items have sentimental value to you before selling them.

11

RESPONSIBLE CREDIT CARD MANAGEMENT

Managing your credit cards responsibly is essential for maintaining good financial health and avoiding debt problems. Here are some tips for managing your credit cards responsibly:

1. Know your limits: Make sure you know the credit limit on your card and do not exceed it. If you exceed your limit, you could face over-limit fees and damage your credit score.
2. Pay on time: It is important to make your monthly payments on time to avoid late fees and protect your credit score. Consider setting up automatic payments or setting reminders to make sure you don't forget to make your payments on time.
3. Keep a low balance: Try to keep the balance on your credit card as low as possible. If you carry a high balance, you could face high-interest charges and damage your credit score.
4. Be selective with your purchases: Don't use your credit cards for unnecessary purchases or luxuries that you can't afford. Try to use them only for essential expenses and stay within your budget.
5. Review your statements: Review your monthly statements to make sure there are no incorrect or unexpected charges.

6. Don't borrow more than you can afford to pay back: Make sure you can pay back the money you are borrowing. Don't borrow more than you can afford to pay back, as you could face debt problems.

In summary, to manage your credit cards responsibly, it is important to know your limits, pay on time, keep a low balance, be selective with your purchases, review your statements, and not borrow more than you can afford to pay back.

Part III
Finding Employment or Starting a Business

12

IDENTIFYING PERSONAL SKILLS AND STRENGTHS

Identifying personal skills and strengths is essential for finding a suitable job or starting a successful business. This will allow you to focus on jobs or business opportunities that match your skills and strengths.

1. Job search: Identify job opportunities online, through networking, or by searching job pages on the internet. It is important to research companies and jobs before applying to ensure they fit your skills and personal goals.
2. Establish a business plan: If you want to start a business, it is essential to establish a solid business plan. This includes researching the market, defining business goals, identifying necessary resources, and establishing a marketing strategy.
3. Obtain financing: If you need financing to start a business, research available financing options. You can seek financing through banks, investors, or online loans. It is also important to establish a solid financial plan that includes the business budget and operating expenses.
4. Build a personal brand: Creating a strong personal brand can help you find a job or attract clients for your business. This includes establishing an online presence, creating an

attractive resume or professional website, and building a network of contacts.

5. Develop skills and knowledge: To succeed in the job or business market, it is important to continue developing relevant skills and knowledge. This can include professional training, attending events and conferences, reading specialized books and articles, or seeking mentors.
6. Be persistent and proactive: Finding a job or starting a successful business can be a difficult and frustrating process. It is important to be persistent, proactive, and maintain a positive attitude throughout the process.

How to identify personal skills and strengths:

1. Self-assessment: It is important to perform a self-assessment to identify your personal skills and strengths. Consider your technical skills and interpersonal skills.
2. Seek feedback: Asking for feedback from friends, family, or colleagues can help you identify skills and strengths that you may not have noticed.
3. Take a personality test: Taking a personality test can help you identify your strengths and weaknesses and understand how you relate to others.
4. Identify your interests: Identifying your interests and hobbies can help you discover skills and strengths you didn't know you had.
5. Analyze your achievements: Analyzing your past achievements can help you identify skills and strengths that you used to achieve them.
6. Observe the strengths of others: Observing the strengths of successful people you admire can help you identify skills and strengths you would like to develop.

7. Seek opportunities to develop skills: Seeking opportunities to develop skills can help you discover skills and strengths you didn't know you had.
8. Practice and improve your skills: Practicing and improving your skills can help you identify skills and strengths you may not have noticed before.

Format for identifying personal skills:

1. Technical skills:

- Knowledge of specialized software
- Ability to work with hand tools
- Ability to program in a certain programming language.

2. Interpersonal skills:

- Ability to listen and communicate effectively
- Ability to work in a team
- Ability to lead and motivate others.

3. Creative skills:

- Ability to create visual content
- Ability to write persuasive texts
- Ability to generate new ideas.

4. Problem-solving skills:

- Ability to analyze data and make informed decisions
- Ability to effectively solve complex problems
- Ability to identify patterns and trends.

5. Organizational skills:

- Ability to plan and coordinate projects
- Ability to set priorities and manage time effectively

- Ability to maintain an organized and orderly work environment.

Remember that this is just a sample and that you can customize it to include your specific personal skills and strengths. The goal is to identify your skills and strengths to use them in achieving your personal and professional goals.

Self-Assessment Format:

1. Technical skills:

- What technical skills do I have in my work area?
- What technical skills do I need to improve?
- How can I improve my technical skills?

2. Interpersonal skills:

- How do I relate to my colleagues and coworkers?
- How do I handle conflicts and difficult situations?
- How can I improve my ability to communicate effectively?

3. Creative skills:

- How do I use my creativity in my daily work?
- How can I use my creativity more effectively?
- How can I foster a more creative work environment?

4. Problem-solving skills:

- How do I handle problematic situations in my work?
- How can I improve my ability to analyze and solve problems effectively?
- How can I learn to make informed decisions in my work?

5. Organizational skills:

- How do I manage my time and set priorities?

- How can I improve my ability to plan and coordinate projects?
- How can I maintain an organized and orderly work environment? Remember that this format is just an example, and you can customize it to include the personal skills and strengths that are important to your work and personal goals.

The objective is to evaluate your skills objectively to identify areas for improvement and establish action plans to achieve your goals.

13

JOB SEARCH

How to search for job opportunities:

1. Identify your skills and strengths: Identifying your skills and strengths will help you focus your job search on roles that best fit your abilities.
2. Update your resume: Make sure your resume is up to date and focused on your relevant skills and work experience.
3. Create an online profile: Creating a profile on LinkedIn and other online professional networks can help you connect with employers and make your profile more visible.
4. Search for job postings online: Search for job postings online on job websites and on the website of the company you would like to work for.
5. Attend job fairs: Attending job fairs is a good way to meet employers and search for job opportunities.
6. Request referrals: Requesting referrals from friends, family, or former colleagues can help you find job opportunities and connect with employers.
7. Contact employers directly: Contacting employers directly that interest you can help you obtain information about potential job opportunities.
8. Work with a staffing agency: Working with a staffing agency can help you find job opportunities that may otherwise go unnoticed.

Here is an example of a resume format:

Full Name Address Phone Email

Summary: This is where you should make a brief introduction of yourself and your professional skills. You can include information such as your professional title, years of experience, key skills, and notable accomplishments.

Work Experience:

1. Job Title / Company Name / Location / Dates of Employment

- Description of key responsibilities and achievements in the role.

2. Job Title / Company Name / Location / Dates of Employment

- Description of key responsibilities and achievements in the role.

Education:

1. Degree Title / Institution / Graduation Date

- Description of relevant coursework and academic achievements.

2. Degree Title / Institution / Graduation Date

- Description of relevant coursework and academic achievements.

Skills and Knowledge:

- List of relevant skills and technical knowledge.

References:

- List of professional contacts who can provide references.

Remember that your resume should be easy to read and organized logically. Use bullet points and bold text to highlight important points. Also, make sure your contact information is up to date and easy to find.

Here are some staffing agency websites that may be useful:

1. Indeed: It is one of the most popular job search websites. It offers a wide variety of jobs in different industries and locations.
2. LinkedIn: It is a professional social network that also has a jobs section. Users can search for and apply to jobs directly on the platform.
3. Glassdoor: In addition to job listings, it also provides company information and previous employee reviews.
4. Monster: It is another popular job search website that offers a wide variety of jobs in different industries.
5. ZipRecruiter: It uses a search algorithm to connect job seekers with jobs that best fit their skills and experience.
6. CareerBuilder: It offers a wide variety of jobs in different industries and also provides tools for improving resumes and job searches.

Remember that it is also important to search on specific company and organization websites and make use of social networks to connect with professionals and employers in your field of interest.

14

ESTABLISHING A BUSINESS PLAN

1. Identifying the Business Idea: Identifying the business idea is the first step in developing a business plan. Make sure you have a clear understanding of what you want to achieve with your business.
2. Market Research: Market research is essential in determining if there is a need for your product or service and to understand your potential customers.
3. Define Your Target Audience: Defining your target audience will help you focus your marketing efforts and develop specific strategies to attract and retain your customers.
4. Analyze the Competition: Analyzing the competition can help you identify strengths and weaknesses in your business idea and develop strategies to stand out in the market.
5. Develop a Marketing Strategy: Developing a marketing strategy is essential in attracting and retaining customers. Make sure you have a solid and well-thought-out strategy.
6. Establish a Financial Plan: Establishing a financial plan will help you determine the viability of your business idea and set a budget for the startup and growth of your business.
7. Create an Operations Plan: Creating an operations plan will help you define how your business will operate and develop

efficient processes for production, customer service, and employee management.

8. Establish a Contingency Plan: Establishing a contingency plan will help you be prepared for any unexpected situations that may affect your business.

Example of a simple business plan, which includes the basic elements mentioned above:

- Executive Summary: In this section, a brief description of the business, its products or services, long-term goals, and plans to achieve those goals are presented.

- Market Analysis: In this section, the market is analyzed, potential customers are identified, competition is evaluated, and growth opportunities are identified.

- Products and Services: In this section, the product or service offered is described, its unique value is explained, and how it differentiates from the competition is explained.

- Marketing Strategy: In this section, the marketing strategy that will be used to reach potential customers, including marketing channels and plans to promote the business, is described.

- Financial Plan: In this section, the start-up costs, expected revenues, and projected cash flow are established. The budget and funding sources are also described.

- Operations and Management: In this section, the daily operations of the business, how it will be managed, and who will be responsible for its management are described.

- Contingency Plan: In this section, the contingency plans in case of unexpected situations that may affect the business are described.

Example of a Business Plan:

Business Plan for ZapatoLandia:

1. Executive Summary:

- ZapatoLandia is a company dedicated to the production and sale of high-quality footwear.
- We offer a wide range of footwear models for men and women between 24 and 60 years old.
- Our long-term goal is to grow and develop over 500 footwear models to meet the needs of our customers.
- With more than 20 years of experience in high-quality leather and footwear, our team is committed to offering high-quality and comfortable footwear.
- Our competitive advantage is our combination of quality, design, and affordable price.
- The footwear market in our area is stable, and there is an increase in demand for high-quality products.

2. Market Analysis:

- The footwear market in our area is valued at X million dollars, and an annual growth of X% is expected in the next 5 years.
- ZapatoLandia's target audience is men and women between 24 and 60 years old who seek quality and comfort at affordable prices.
- The main competitors in the footwear market are A, B, and C, but our competitive advantage allows us to differentiate ourselves from them.

- Our pricing strategy is based on offering high-quality products at affordable prices.

3. Products and Services:

- Zapato Landia offers a wide range of footwear models for men and women, including casual, formal, athletic, and special occasion shoes.
- All of our products are designed and manufactured with high-quality materials to ensure comfort and durability.

4. Marketing Strategy:

- Our marketing strategy is based on advertising on social media, advertising in local newspapers, and participating in local footwear fairs.
- We also offer discounts and promotions to incentivize repeat purchases and customer loyalty.
- Financial Plan: We expect to generate annual revenues of X million dollars in the first year, and a growth of X% in the next 5 years.
- Our cost structure includes the cost of materials, production costs, marketing expenses, and overhead expenses.
- We expect to finance our company through external investors and loans.

5. Operations and Management:

- Zapato Landia has a highly trained team with over 20 years of experience in the production and sale of footwear.
- Our operations include footwear production, inventory management, sales in physical and online stores, and customer service.

6. Contingency Plan:

- Our contingency plan includes strategies to deal with competition, changes in industry trends, and unexpected situations that may affect our business.

Here is a possible marketing strategy for Zapato Landia:

1. Identify the target audience: The first step in the marketing strategy is to identify the target audience. In the case of ZapatoLandia, the brand targets people between 24 and 60 years old who are looking for high-quality footwear.
2. Positioning: ZapatoLandia must highlight its unique strengths in the footwear market, such as the quality of its products and the wide variety of models available. This will help the brand differentiate itself from its competitors and attract customers who are looking for these benefits.
3. Creating an online presence: An online presence is essential in the marketing strategy of any company today. Zapato Landia must ensure it has an attractive and easy-to-use website, and may also consider creating profiles on social media platforms like Facebook and Instagram to reach a wider audience.
4. Advertising in traditional media: Although advertising in traditional media such as television and newspapers has lost some strength in recent years, it can still be effective in reaching a wide audience. Zapato Landia may consider placing ads in local or regional media to attract potential customers.
5. Content marketing: Creating relevant and useful content can be an effective way to attract customers to the brand. Zapato Landia may consider creating a blog on its website with tips on shoe care, fashion trends, and other topics relevant to its target audience.

6. Promotional events: Zapato Landia can organize promotional events, such as special sales or footwear fairs, to attract customers and increase brand awareness. These events can be announced on the brand's website and social media.
7. Loyalty program: Implementing a loyalty program can be an effective way to retain existing customers and attract new ones. Zapato Landia may consider offering exclusive discounts, special offers, and other benefits to loyalty program members.

Remember that any marketing strategy should be tailored to the specific needs and objectives of the brand and should be flexible to adapt to changes in the market and customer needs.

Conducting a Market Study is very important.

To conduct a market study, follow these steps:

1. Define the study objective: Before starting the study, you must clearly define the study objective. What do you want to know about the market? What is the problem or opportunity you want to explore?
2. Define your target audience: To carry out the study, you must define which group of people you want to reach. This will allow you to focus on relevant information and obtain more accurate results.
3. Identify sources of information: It is important that you identify the sources of information that you will use for the study. You can use surveys, interviews, focus groups, sales data, competition analysis, and any other source that you consider relevant.

4. Design the questionnaire or interview guide: If you are going to use surveys or interviews to collect information, you should design a questionnaire or interview guide that includes specific questions related to the study objective.
5. Collect data: Once you have defined your sources of information and designed your questionnaire or interview guide, you should proceed to collect data. You can conduct surveys or interviews in person, via email, phone, social media, or any other appropriate means.
6. Analyze data: Once you have collected the data, you should carefully analyze it to identify relevant patterns and trends. You can use tools such as tables, charts, and statistics to facilitate the analysis.
7. Make decisions: Finally, you should use the information obtained to make informed decisions about the market and your product or service. Use the information to identify opportunities, solve problems, and improve your offering. Remember that market research is a continuous process and that you should update it periodically to keep it relevant and up-to-date.

Here is an example of a market research study for a new café in an urban area:

Objective of the study: To evaluate the demand and preferences of consumers regarding a new café in the city center.

Data collection method: Online and in-person surveys of 300 people from the urban area.

Results:

1. Demographics: 60% of respondents were women and 40% were men. 70% of respondents were between 25 and 45

years old, 20% were over 45 years old, and 10% were under 25 years old.

2. Coffee consumption frequency: 70% of respondents consumed coffee at least once a day, 20% consumed it several times a week, and 10% consumed it less than once a week.
3. Coffee preferences: 60% of respondents preferred black coffee, 30% preferred coffee with milk, and 10% preferred other options.
4. Food options: 80% of respondents indicated that they would like to have healthy food options, such as salads and sandwiches, while 20% preferred more indulgent options, such as desserts and cakes.
5. Price: 60% of respondents indicated that they would be willing to pay between $3 and $5 for a cup of coffee, while 40% would be willing to pay more than $5.

Conclusions: The results indicate a solid demand for a new café in the city center, with a strong preference for black coffee and healthy food options. Most respondents would be willing to pay reasonable prices for their coffee, suggesting an opportunity to establish a quality café with competitive prices in the urban area.

15

OBTAINING FINANCING

How to obtain financing for your business:

1. Bank loans: Bank loans are one of the most common forms of financing for businesses. You can go to your local bank and apply for a loan that suits your needs.
2. External investors: External investors, such as angel investors or venture capital funds, can provide financing in exchange for a stake in your business. You must be prepared to present a solid business plan and convince investors that your business has the potential to be profitable.
3. Crowdfunding: Crowdfunding is a form of financing in which money is raised through an online platform, usually through individual donations. To be successful in crowdfunding, it is important to have a well-designed and persuasive marketing campaign.
4. Microloans: Microloans are small loans granted to small business owners and entrepreneurs who do not have access to traditional financing. Microloans are usually granted by non-profit organizations and do not require collateral.
5. Government financing programs: In many countries, there are government financing programs that are intended to support small and medium-sized businesses.

Applying for a bank loan may vary slightly from one bank to another, but generally the steps you should follow are as follows:

I. Research different loan options: Before applying for a loan, it is important to research different options and compare interest rates, terms, and conditions of each one. This will allow you to select the loan that best suits your needs.

II. Prepare your documents: To apply for a loan, you must have your personal and financial documentation in order. Generally, you will need your official identification, proof of address, proof of income, and bank statements.

III. Schedule an appointment with the bank: Once you have chosen the loan you want to apply for and have all your documentation in order, you should schedule an appointment with a bank representative. You can do this online or by phone.

IV. Submit your application: During the appointment with the bank representative, you will need to submit your loan application and provide the required documentation. The bank representative will review your application and inform you if you qualify for the loan.

V. Wait for the bank's response: After submitting your application, you will need to wait for the bank to inform you whether your loan has been approved or not. This process can take a few days or weeks, depending on the bank and the type of loan.

VI. Sign the contract: If your loan has been approved, you will need to sign the loan contract and agree to the terms and conditions of the loan. Make sure to carefully read the contract before signing it and understand all the clauses and terms.

VII. Use the loan responsibly: Once you have obtained the loan, it is important to use it responsibly and make payments on time to avoid additional charges and damage to your credit history.

Remember that each bank may have its own requirements and processes for applying for a loan, so it is important to inform yourself and follow the specific instructions of each financial institution.

Part IV
Establishing Financial Goals

16

DEFINING REALISTIC AND ACHIEVABLE FINANCIAL GOALS

Financial goals are specific and measurable targets that you set to achieve a desired financial position. To make financial goals realistic and achievable, they must meet certain criteria. Below are some tips for defining realistic and achievable financial goals:

1. Be specific: Set specific and measurable financial goals. For example, instead of saying "I want to save money," set a goal with a specific amount you want to save.

Here is an example format for setting specific and measurable financial goals:

Financial goal: Saving for an emergency fund

Target amount: $5,000

Timeframe: 12 months

Action plan:

- Review expenses and look for areas to reduce costs
- Save $417 per month for the next 12 months
- Set up a separate account for the emergency fund and deposit the money there monthly

- Regularly review progress and make adjustments if necessary.

This is just an example, but you can adapt this format to any specific financial goal you have. Remember to be as detailed as possible and make sure it's measurable so you can see if you're achieving your goal.

2. Be realistic: It's important that goals are realistic and achievable. Don't set financial goals that are out of your reach or require superhuman effort to achieve.
3. Set deadlines: Financial goals should have a specific timeframe to be achieved. For example, if your goal is to save for a vacation, set a specific date for the trip and establish a deadline to save the necessary money for the trip.
4. Make a plan: Once you've set your financial goals, it's important to make a plan to achieve them. The plan should include the necessary steps to achieve the goal, as well as a timeline to complete each step.
5. Review and adjust: Regularly review your progress and adjust your plan if necessary. If you're not progressing as planned, it may be necessary to adjust your plan or financial goals.

In summary, to set realistic and achievable financial goals, you must be specific, realistic, set deadlines, make a plan, and regularly review and adjust your progress.

17

PRIORITIZING FINANCIAL GOALS

In order to prioritize your financial goals, you must evaluate their importance and establish a priority order. Here are some tips for prioritizing financial goals:

1. List your financial goals: Make a list of all your financial goals and prioritize them in order of importance.

Here is an example format for setting financial goals:

Financial goal: [Brief description of financial goal] Example: Save for an emergency fund

Target amount: [Amount in dollars you want to reach] Example: $5,000

Timeframe: [Period of time you want to achieve your goal] Example: 12 months

Action plan:

- [Detailed description of the specific steps you will take to achieve your goal, including monthly savings, expense reduction, investment in the market, etc.]
- Example: Save $417 per month for the next 12 months
- Set up a separate account for the emergency fund and deposit the money there monthly

- Regularly review progress and make adjustments if necessary

Target date: [Date you expect to achieve your goal]

Example: December 31, 2023

Progress monitoring: [How you will measure and monitor your progress towards achieving your goal] Example: Check my savings account balance every month and make adjustments to my action plan as necessary

This is just an example format for setting financial goals. You can customize it according to your specific needs and financial goals. It is important to be specific and realistic when setting your financial goals to ensure that they are achievable and measurable.

2. Evaluate their urgency: Evaluate the urgency of each goal. If a goal is critical, such as paying off overdue debt or avoiding interest charges, then it should have a high priority.
3. Consider the deadlines: If there is a deadline for achieving a financial goal, make sure to take it into account when setting its priority. For example, if you want to save for a down payment on a car, you may want to set a deadline to achieve it before the deadline to get a good offer.
4. Adjust according to your personal circumstances: Adjust the priority order according to your personal circumstances. For example, if you have an unstable income, you may want to prioritize creating an emergency fund over paying off a high-interest debt.
5. Make a plan: Once you have established the priority order of your financial goals, make a plan to achieve them. The

plan should include the necessary steps to achieve each goal, as well as a calendar to complete each step.

In summary, to prioritize your financial goals, list your goals, evaluate their urgency, consider the deadlines, adjust according to your personal circumstances, and make a plan to achieve them.

18

MAINTAINING FOCUS ON LONG-TERM GOALS

Maintaining focus on long-term goals refers to the ability to stay committed and motivated to achieving financial goals in the long run, even when there are distractions, temptations, or short-term difficulties that may derail us from the path. It is important to have a clear and concrete vision of what one wants to achieve in the long term and focus on the necessary steps to achieve it, without losing sight of the ultimate goal. This requires discipline, patience, and perseverance, and can be aided by creating a detailed financial plan that includes specific milestones and deadlines to measure progress towards long-term goals. Staying focused on long-term goals can also be aided by regularly reviewing the financial plan and updating it as needed. Please note that this example is only a guide and should be customized to your own specific financial needs and goals. Example of Financial Plan

1. Financial goal: Save $50,000 for a down payment on a house in 5 years.
2. Milestones:

- Save $10,000 in the first year
- Save $20,000 in the second year
- Save $30,000 in the third year

- Save $40,000 in the fourth year Reach the $50,000 goal in the fifth year.

3. Saving strategies:

- Reduce non-essential expenses (such as dining out and entertainment).
- Set a detailed monthly budget and stick to it.
- Increase income by working overtime or seeking additional jobs
- Automatically save a fixed amount each month.

4. Investments:

- Invest a portion of savings in high-yield savings accounts
- Consider investing in the stock market through index funds.

5. Measuring progress:

- Review savings balances and expenses each month to ensure on track to reach established milestones.
- Track credit score to ensure it stays at a healthy level to obtain the best possible interest rate on the mortgage loan.

6. Specific deadlines:

- Save $10,000 by the end of year 1
- Save $20,000 by the end of year 2
- Save $30,000 by the end of year 3
- Save $40,000 by the end of year 4
- Reach the $50,000 goal by the end of year 5.

7. Contingency plan:

- If a financial emergency arises that affects the ability to save, adjust the monthly budget accordingly to ensure staying on track to reach long-term goals.

  Remember that this is just an example of a financial plan and should be customized to your own specific financial needs and goals.

I provide you with an example format for a detailed financial plan that includes specific milestones and timelines to measure progress towards long-term goals.

Below is a simple model:

Format for a detailed financial plan that includes specific milestones and timelines:

1. Financial Goal: [Brief description of financial goal]

   Example: Save $20,000 for a down payment on a house in 3 years

2. Milestones:

- Save $5,000 by end of year 1
- Save $10,000 by end of year 2
- Save $15,000 by end of year 3
- Reach goal of $20,000 by end of year 3

3. Saving Strategies:

- Reduce unnecessary expenses (e.g., dining out, entertainment)
- Establish a detailed monthly budget and stick to it
- Increase income by working overtime or taking on additional work

- Automatically save a fixed amount each month

4. Investments:

- Invest a portion of savings in high-yield savings accounts
- Consider investing in the stock market through index funds

5. Progress Measurement:

- Review savings balances and expenses each month to ensure on track to reach established milestones
- Monitor credit score to ensure it stays at a healthy level for best possible interest rate on mortgage loan

6. Specific Timelines:

- Save $5,000 by end of year 1
- Save $10,000 by end of year 2
- Save $15,000 by end of year 3
- Reach goal of $20,000 by end of year 3

7. Contingency Plan:

   If a financial emergency arises that impacts ability to save, adjust monthly budget accordingly to stay on track towards long-term goals.

It is important that this format be customized and adapted to the specific needs and objectives of each person or company. Additionally, it is important to remember that the financial plan should be regularly reviewed and adjusted as necessary to ensure that the established milestones and timelines towards long-term goals are being met.

Note: Milestones are specific goals or achievements that must be reached along the way to meet the long-term financial objective.

They are important because they help break down the goal into manageable parts and measure progress along the way to achieving the ultimate goal.

For example, if the long-term financial goal is to save for retirement, a milestone could be to reach a certain savings level by the age of 30, another milestone could be to reach another savings level by the age of 40, and so on.

Each milestone represents a step towards the ultimate goal of a well-funded retirement.

Part V

Tips for Attitude and Motivation

19

CULTIVATING CONFIDENCE, RESILIENCE, AND PERSEVERANCE

Cultivating confidence, resilience, and perseverance is fundamental to achieving financial and personal success. Self-confidence is key to making important decisions and persisting despite difficulties. Resilience, on the other hand, is the ability to adapt and overcome difficult situations. And finally, perseverance is the attitude of not giving up on obstacles and staying on course towards long-term goals.

To cultivate confidence, it is important to recognize one's strengths and abilities, as well as to identify areas that need improvement. Through financial education and constant practice, confidence in financial decision-making can be increased.

Resilience can be developed through exposure to difficult situations and adopting a mindset of learning and growth. Learning to manage stress and pressure is also essential to developing resilience.

Resilience refers to a person's ability to face and overcome difficult situations, whether economic, personal, emotional, or social. In other words, it is the ability to adapt and recover from adversity. Resilience does not mean that one does not feel pain or stress in a difficult situation, but rather that they have the ability to overcome and recover from it, learning from the experience and emerging stronger.

Perseverance can be strengthened through clear definition of long-term goals and the development of an action plan with specific timelines and milestones. Maintaining motivation and focus on goals, even when facing obstacles and setbacks, is essential to cultivating perseverance.

Together, confidence, resilience, and perseverance can help face economic and personal challenges more successfully and achieve a healthy and prosperous financial life.

20

IDENTIFICATION AND OVERCOMING PERSONAL FEARS AND LIMITATIONS

Identifying and overcoming personal fears and limitations is a process that may require time and effort, but it is essential to achieve financial and personal success. Here are some steps you can follow to identify and overcome your personal fears and limitations:

1. Identify your fears and limitations: The first step in overcoming your personal fears and limitations is to recognize them. Ask yourself what is holding you back, what fears you have, and what limitations you feel are preventing you from moving forward.

   To identify your fears, you need to answer these questions:

   a. What is the origin of my fear? Is it based on previous experiences or is it something that is in my imagination?
   b. What is the worst that could happen if I face my fear? Is this concern realistic or exaggerated?
   c. What opportunities am I missing out on by not facing my fear? What could I gain if I overcome my fear?
   d. What resources do I have available to face my fear? Is there someone I can trust to help me?
   e. How can I begin to take steps to overcome my fear? What is the first step I should take?

f. How can I stay motivated and perseverant while working to overcome my fear?

Answering these questions will help you identify the roots of your fear and create an action plan to overcome it. It will also allow you to change your perspective on your fears and see them as opportunities to grow and move forward rather than obstacles.

2. Understand your fears and limitations: Once you have identified your fears and limitations, try to understand them better. Where do they come from? Are they realistic or based on false assumptions? What effect are they having on your life and finances?
3. Set realistic goals: Once you have identified and understood your fears and limitations, set realistic goals to overcome them. Ask yourself what actions you can take to face your fears and overcome your limitations. For example, if you are afraid of investing, you can start by investing small amounts of money to gain experience and confidence.

   Here are some actions you can take to face your fears:

   a. Face your fear: Often, the only way to overcome a fear is to face it directly. This can be difficult, but it is essential to overcome your fears. If you are afraid of public speaking, for example, look for opportunities to practice speaking in public, such as in small meetings or community events.
   b. Investigate your fear: Investigate your fear to better understand it. Ignorance can often make fears seem bigger and insurmountable. By investigating your fear, you can gain a better understanding of its origin and learn ways to face it.

c. Learn new skills: If your fear is related to a lack of skills, look for ways to develop those skills. For example, if you are afraid of swimming, you can take swimming lessons to learn how to swim and increase your confidence.
d. Seek support: Seek support from friends, family, or a trained professional to help you overcome your fears. Talking to someone who understands your fears can help you feel more secure and confident.
e. Practice relaxation: Anxiety can exacerbate fears, so it is important to learn relaxation techniques such as deep breathing, meditation, or yoga. These techniques can help you manage anxiety and face your fears with a clearer mind.
f. Visualize success: Visualize success and try to imagine yourself overcoming your fear. This can help you feel more confident and prepared to face the fear.
g. Celebrate your achievements: Every small step you take to face your fear is an important achievement. Celebrate your achievements and remind yourself that you are strong and capable of overcoming your fear.

4. Seek support:

Overcoming your fears and limitations can be a difficult process, so it's important to seek support. Talk to trusted friends, family, or a financial advisor about your goals and challenges. Additionally, you can join online support groups or attend training and personal development events to connect with others who are working on their own personal challenges.

5. Take action:

   Once you have set goals and sought support, it's important to take action to overcome your fears and limitations. Start with small steps and celebrate your achievements.

   Over time, each small victory will help you overcome your fears and limitations and achieve the financial and personal Independence you desire.

Developing a positive and proactive attitude can be key to overcoming challenges and achieving financial goals. Here are some tips to develop this attitude:

1. Learn to see opportunities in every situation: Instead of focusing on what you can't do, always look for alternatives and solutions to reach your goals.
2. Be optimistic: Even when things don't go as planned, try to always see the positive side and think that you can learn something from every experience.
3. Surround yourself with positive people: People with a positive attitude can influence your mood and motivate you to move forward. Look for people who support and motivate you.
4. Celebrate your achievements: Recognize your achievements and celebrate every step you take towards your goals. This will help you maintain a positive attitude and keep moving forward.

Celebrating your achievements is an important part of the process of reaching your goals. Here are some tips on how you can celebrate your achievements:

a. Recognize your achievements: The first thing you need to do is recognize your achievements and realize what you have accomplished. Don't belittle yourself or your achievements, strive to appreciate and recognize what you have achieved.

b. Celebrate your achievements: Celebrate your achievements in the way you prefer, whether it's with a dinner, a party, a trip, a gift for yourself, or simply dedicating time to do something you enjoy.

c. Share your achievements: Share your achievements with friends, family, colleagues and people close to you. Ask them to congratulate and celebrate with you, and if you can invite them to share the celebration, even better!

d. Reflect on your progress: Reflect on the path you have taken to achieve your goals. Think about the challenges and obstacles you have overcome and how you have learned and grown in the process.

e. Take a break: After celebrating your achievements, take some time to rest and recharge before continuing to work on your next goals. Remember that celebrating your achievements is an important part of the process of reaching your goals. Celebration helps you stay motivated and focused on the path to success and gives you the opportunity to recognize and value your achievements along the way.

5. Take action: Instead of being paralyzed by fear or indecision, take action and do something to move towards your goals. Action will take you closer to your objectives and help you stay motivated and positive.

Remember that developing a positive and proactive attitude is a process that requires practice and perseverance, but that can make a big difference in your financial and personal life.

22

LEARNING FROM MISTAKES AND FAILURES

Learning from mistakes and failures is an important part of the personal and financial growth process. Often, when we make mistakes or fail at something, we tend to feel bad and believe that we have failed. However, it is important to remember that mistakes and failures are opportunities to learn and improve.

One of the keys to learning from mistakes and failures is to reflect on what happened and try to understand why things did not turn out as expected. Did we do something wrong? Was it a planning or execution problem? Was there something we could not anticipate?

Once we have identified the causes of mistakes or failures, we can start working on solutions to prevent them from happening again in the future. This may include implementing new systems, adopting best practices, or undergoing additional training.

It is important to remember that learning from mistakes and failures is an ongoing process. We must be willing to accept that we will sometimes make mistakes and fail, but we must also be committed to learning from them and continuously improving.

Part VI

Inspirational stories of overcoming financial struggles

23

STORIES OF PEOPLE WHO OVERCAME THEIR ECONOMIC CRISES AND ACHIEVED SUCCESS.

Here are some inspiring stories of economic overcoming:

1. Walt Disney: One of the most successful entertainment creators of all time, Walt Disney faced several financial failures before finding success. He was fired from a job at a newspaper for "lack of imagination" and his first animation studio failed. But Walt didn't give up, and eventually created an entertainment empire that included theme parks, movies, television, and much more.
2. J.K. Rowling: Harry Potter author J.K. Rowling struggled with extreme poverty before becoming one of the world's most successful writers. Rowling was a single mother and relied on welfare checks to survive while writing her first novel. But her perseverance and dedication led her to success, and today she is one of the world's most beloved and successful authors.
3. Oprah Winfrey: Famous television host Oprah Winfrey overcame a difficult and poor childhood to become one of the world's most powerful and wealthy women. She was sexually abused as a child and her childhood was marked by poverty and family instability. But Oprah persevered and

worked hard, becoming a highly successful television host, entrepreneur, and philanthropist.

4. Jeff Bezos: Amazon founder Jeff Bezos went through several failures before finding success in business. He founded a software company that failed, and his first online book-selling company took several years to achieve success. But Bezos persevered and worked hard, and eventually turned Amazon into one of the most successful companies in the world.
5. Tony Robbins: Famous motivational speaker Tony Robbins grew up in a poor and abusive family. At 17, he left home and started working as a janitor. But his entrepreneurial spirit led him to become a successful businessman, writer, and motivational speaker, helping millions of people achieve their goals and improve their lives.
6. Vera Wang: Famous fashion designer Vera Wang started her career as a figure skater, but decided to pursue a career in fashion after failing to make it to the Olympics. After working as a fashion editor at Vogue, Wang opened her own bridal boutique, but faced financial difficulties. Instead of giving up, she focused on improving her offerings and expanding her brand, becoming one of the most successful fashion designers in the world.
7. Warren Buffett: One of the most successful investors of all time, Warren Buffett started his career as a newspaper delivery boy and tax collector. After investing in several companies, Buffett became a billionaire, but never forgot his humble origins. He continues to be one of the most generous philanthropists in the world, committed to giving away most of his fortune to charity.
8. Steve Jobs: Apple co-founder Steve Jobs was adopted and grew up in a working-class family. After dropping out of

college, Jobs worked as a technician at Atari before co-founding Apple in his garage. Despite several failures and challenges, Jobs remained focused on his vision and revolutionized the technology industry.

9. J.K. Simmons: Oscar-winning actor J.K. Simmons spent years struggling to make a career in Hollywood. He worked in several odd jobs, including teaching music and acting in regional theater before finding success in film and television.
10. Sarah Blakely: Spanx founder Sarah Blakely spent years working in sales before creating the world's most famous line of underwear and hosiery. Despite a lack of experience in the fashion industry, Blakely persevered and built a billion-dollar business empire.

These are just some of the many inspiring stories of economic overcoming. Each of these individuals overcame challenges and failures to find success, demonstrating that perseverance, determination, and hard work can lead to great achievements and overcome economic difficulties.

24

INSPIRATIONAL LESSONS AND ADVICE FROM SUCCESSFUL PEOPLE

There are many successful people who have left inspiring lessons and advice that can help us in our own pursuit of financial success. Here are some examples:

1. Warren Buffett: "If you cannot control your emotions, you cannot control your money." It's important to stay calm and not be swayed by fear or greed when it comes to making financial decisions.
2. Tony Robbins: "Success in life is the sum of right decisions and wrong decisions made along the way." Sometimes we fail, but it's important to learn from our mistakes and move forward.
3. Oprah Winfrey: "Do what you love and the money will follow." If we follow our passions and work hard, financial success can follow.
4. Elon Musk: "If something is important enough, even if the odds are against you, you should still do it." Sometimes taking risks is necessary to achieve financial success.
5. Richard Branson: "I've always believed that if you enjoy what you do, the money will come." If we enjoy what we do and are motivated, we are more likely to reach our financial goals.

6. Steve Jobs: "Innovation distinguishes between a leader and a follower." If we want to achieve financial success, it's important to think outside the box and find new ways to approach problems.

25

INTERVIEWS WITH PEOPLE WHO HAVE OVERCOME MAJOR ECONOMIC CHALLENGES.

Interview with John Paul Dejoria (Co-founder of Patron Tequila)

John Paul DeJoria, founder of Paul Mitchell and co-founder of Patron Tequila, grew up in poverty and faced many challenges in his life. In an interview with Forbes, DeJoria talked about how he overcame poverty and became a successful entrepreneur.

According to DeJoria, the key to his success was his mentality and positive attitude. Despite the challenges he faced, DeJoria never lost hope or faith in himself. He also talked about the importance of having a clear vision and purpose in life, and working hard and persevering to achieve goals.

Furthermore, DeJoria highlighted the importance of giving and helping others. Throughout his career, he has supported a number of charitable causes and used his success to help others achieve their goals.

In summary, John Paul DeJoria overcame poverty and achieved success thanks to his positive mentality, clear vision and purpose in life, hard work and perseverance, and his commitment to giving and helping others.

Interview with Suze Orman (Financial Expert)

In an interview with The New York Times, Suze Orman talked about her own experience of overcoming poverty and debt, and how she became a financial expert. Orman highlighted the importance of being aware of your finances and making informed decisions about money.

Orman talked about how she came to the conclusion that financial decisions are based on emotions and how it is important to understand how our emotions influence our financial decisions. She also talked about the importance of having a budget and how following a budget can help us make informed financial decisions.

Furthermore, Orman highlighted the importance of having a plan for the future and making informed and well-thought-out investments. She also talked about the importance of being realistic about our finances and not spending more than we can afford.

In summary, Suze Orman talked about the importance of being aware of our finances, making informed and well-thought-out decisions about money, and having a plan for the future. She also highlighted the importance of being realistic about our finances and avoiding spending more than we can afford.

Interview with Daymond John (Founder of FUBU)

In an interview with Inc. magazine, Daymond John, founder of FUBU and a personality on the television show Shark Tank, talked about how he overcame financial challenges and obstacles on the road to success.

John talked about his childhood and how his mother raised him as a single mother. He had to work hard to help support his family, and his experience motivated him to keep working hard to achieve success.

John also talked about the importance of having an entrepreneurial mindset and being creative in seeking solutions to problems. He also highlighted the importance of perseverance and continuing on despite obstacles.

Furthermore, John talked about the importance of education and being willing to learn and grow. He also talked about how surrounding oneself with positive and constructive people can help overcome challenges and achieve success.

In summary, Daymond John talked about how his experience motivated him to work hard to achieve success, the importance of having an entrepreneurial and creative mindset, perseverance, and the importance of education and surrounding oneself with positive people.

Interview with Dave Ramsey (Financial Personality)

In an interview with Money Crashers, Dave Ramsey, author and financial personality, talked about his own experience of overcoming debt and how he has helped others do the same.

Ramsey talked about how he came to the conclusion that he was living beyond his means and how this led to debt. He talked about the importance of being honest with oneself about finances and taking steps to reduce debt and create a budget.

Ramsey also highlighted the importance of financial education and how he has helped millions of people through his books, courses, and radio and television programs. He talked about the importance of being disciplined and staying focused on financial goals.

In addition, Ramsey talked about the importance of being prepared for financial emergencies and having a plan for the future. He also talked about the importance of being generous and giving to others.

In summary, Dave Ramsey spoke about the importance of being honest with oneself about finances, financial education, discipline, being prepared for financial emergencies and the future, and the importance of generosity.

These are some stories of successful people who have overcome the worst and continued with their heads held high until they achieved their dreams.

There are millions of people with these same characteristics, and some of them don't even know they have this same power, the POWER to achieve the impossible.

26

POSITIVE MESSAGES THAT HELP ACHIEVE FINANCIAL SUCCESS.

Motivating and Encouraging Messages

Here are some motivating and encouraging messages that can help you stay focused and motivated on the path to your goals:

"Success is not the key to happiness. Happiness is the key to success. If you love what you're doing, you will be successful." - *Albert Schweitzer*

"Don't give up, every failure is an opportunity to start again with more experience." - *Henry Ford*

"Success is not final, failure is not fatal: it is the courage to continue that counts." - *Winston Churchill*

"The best way to predict your future is to create it." - *Abraham Lincoln*

"Don't wait for opportunities, create them yourself." - *Chris Grosser*

"Success is not the key to happiness. Happiness is the key to success. If you love what you do, you will be successful." - *Herman Cain*

"Success is the sum of small efforts repeated day in and day out." - *Robert Collier*

"The only way to do great work is to love what you do." - *Steve Jobs*

"Failure is simply the opportunity to begin again, this time more intelligently." - *Henry Ford*

"Don't give up, everything worth having takes time and effort." - *Anonymous*

"Success is not the key to happiness. Happiness is the key to success. If you love what you're doing, you will be successful." - *Albert Schweitzer*

"Don't give up, every failure is an opportunity to start again with more experience." - *Henry Ford*

"Success is not final, failure is not fatal: it is the courage to continue that counts." - *Winston Churchill*

"The best way to predict your future is to create it." - *Abraham Lincoln*

"Don't wait for opportunities, create them yourself." - *Chris Grosser*

"Success is not the key to happiness. Happiness is the key to success. If you love what you do, you will be successful." - *Herman Cain*

"Success is the sum of small efforts repeated day in and day out." - *Robert Collier*

"The only way to do great work is to love what you do." - *Steve Jobs*

"Failure is simply the opportunity to begin again, this time more intelligently." - *Henry Ford*

"Don't give up, everything worth having takes time and effort." - *Anonymous*

Remember that each of these motivating and encouraging messages can help you stay focused and motivated on the path to your goals. Find the one that inspires you the most and remember that every small step you take brings you closer to achieving your goals.

You can do this exercise: Choose a maximum of 3 of these motivating phrases and make them yours, you must believe in the phrases you choose and put them into practice.

Mine are:

"Failure is simply the opportunity to begin again, this time more intelligently." - *Henry Ford*

"Success is not the key to happiness. Happiness is the key to success. If you love what you do, you will be successful." - *Herman Cain*

"The best way to predict your future is to create it." - *Abraham Lincoln*

These 3 phrases have helped me achieve what I am doing every day of my life.

27

PERSONAL ANECDOTES AND EXAMPLES.

This is a testimony of a young woman named Ana, who had studied at university and accumulated a large student debt.

Upon graduating, Ana found herself struggling to make her monthly student loan payments and felt trapped in a spiral of debt and financial stress.

Debt control her. Instead, she decided to take steps to pay off her debt as quickly as possible.

She began by setting a strict budget and cutting her expenses as much as possible.

Ana also decided to look for additional jobs to increase her income, working on weekends and evenings after her full-time job.

Ana set a clear goal for herself: to pay off all her student debt within five years.

She worked hard, saved as much as she could, and dedicated all additional income to her student loans.

Despite the challenges and tough times, Ana never lost faith in herself and her ability to pay off her debt.

She remained focused on her goal and never gave up. After five years of hard work and financial sacrifices, Ana managed to completely pay off her student debt.

She felt incredibly proud of her achievement, knowing that she had overcome one of the greatest financial challenges of her life.

Now, Ana lives debt-free and has the financial freedom to pursue her dreams and goals. Her story inspires many others who also struggle with student debt, and shows that with effort and hard work, it is possible to overcome any financial challenge.

This is the story of a man named Carlos, who had worked at the same company for over a decade. Although Carlos was grateful for his job and enjoyed what he did, he had always had the feeling that his true passion was elsewhere: entrepreneurship.

For years, Carlos had ideas for businesses, but had always doubted his ability to carry them out. Finally, after years of working on his idea, he decided to take the leap and start his own business.

Carlos knew that the path to entrepreneurship would not be easy. Leaving his stable and secure job and starting his own business would require a lot of work, time, and financial sacrifices.

But he also knew that if he didn't try, he would always wonder "what if?" After months of careful research and planning, Carlos finally launched his business: an online store selling handmade artisanal products.

Carlos worked tirelessly, dedicating long hours to his business while still working full-time. At first, Carlos encountered many challenges, such as building his website, handling logistics, and finding customers.

But gradually, as his business grew, Carlos began to gain momentum. He began receiving orders from all over the world and making a significant profit.

As his business expanded, Carlos realized that he had found his true passion. He felt more motivated and committed than ever before in his life, and felt incredibly grateful for the opportunity to pursue his dream.

Today, Carlos continues to run his business successfully. Through hard work and perseverance, he has achieved his dream of being a successful entrepreneur.

His story inspires many others to follow their dreams and pursue their true passion in life.

This is Sofia, a woman who had spent most of her life struggling with low income and financial difficulties.

Sofia worked hard in full-time jobs, but despite her efforts, she always seemed to have difficulty making ends meet.

Despite the financial difficulties, Sofia never lost faith in herself and her ability to change her financial situation.

She had always dreamed of achieving financial independence and was determined to do what it takes to achieve her goal.

Sofia started by setting a strict budget, examining every expense and finding ways to reduce her expenses to a minimum.

She began making financial sacrifices, such as avoiding eating out and using public transportation instead of her own car.

But Sofia didn't stop there. She also looked for ways to increase her income, taking on additional jobs in her free time and seeking online entrepreneurial opportunities.

Over time, Sofia began to earn more money and save diligently.

After years of hard work, Sofia finally achieved her goal of financial independence.

Now, she lives a life without financial worries and has the freedom to travel, explore her hobbies, and spend time with her family and friends.

Sofia knows that her financial success was not easy to achieve, but she also knows that hard work and perseverance are worth it.

Her story inspires many people in similar situations, demonstrating that financial independence is possible for those who are willing to work hard and make sacrifices.

The main idea of these stories is that you can follow the same story as Carlos, Ana, Sofia.

You can follow their steps through this book and all its exercises, open your financial mind, and fight for it.

28

THOUGHTS TO AVOID IN YOUR MIND

Negative thoughts that may arise when facing financial challenges, along with some tips for overcoming them:

1. "I don't have enough money to deal with my debts." Instead of focusing on the lack of money, try to find creative solutions to address your debts, such as negotiating payments or looking for opportunities for additional income.
2. "I don't have the necessary skills to succeed in my business." Instead of focusing on your weaknesses, look for ways to develop your skills through courses, training, or business mentoring.
3. "Everything is against me, I can't achieve my goals." Instead of focusing on the difficulties, look for solutions and opportunities to move towards your goals, such as seeking new forms of financing or adapting your business strategy.
4. "I'm not good enough to succeed." Instead of focusing on self-doubt, remember your strengths and past achievements. Seek support from friends and family to remind you of your abilities and capabilities.
5. "I've always been bad with money; I'll never be able to change my financial habits." Instead of focusing on the past, look for solutions to improve your financial habits, such as creating a budget or seeking financial advice.

6. "I can't afford to invest in my future." Instead of focusing on the lack of financial resources, look for creative solutions to invest in your future, such as seeking scholarship opportunities, reducing unnecessary expenses, or seeking financing.
7. "I've always been bad with money, I'll never be financially independent." Instead of focusing on the past, look for solutions to improve your financial skills, such as seeking financial advice or reading books on personal finance.
8. "I'll never be able to get out of debt." Instead of focusing on the magnitude of your debts, look for practical solutions to pay them off, such as debt consolidation or negotiating payments.
9. "I don't have the necessary connections to succeed in business." Instead of focusing on the lack of connections, look for opportunities to expand your professional network, such as attending networking events or seeking business mentors.
10. "I'll never be able to achieve my financial goals, they're too big." Instead of focusing on the magnitude of your goals, break them down into smaller, achievable objectives.

Celebrate each achievement and use your progress as motivation to keep moving forward.

Here are some simple business alternatives for entrepreneurs to put into practice:

1. Cleaning services: A cleaning service business can be an excellent option for entrepreneurs. This type of business can be very profitable and only requires a basic cleaning equipment.
2. Online product sales: Selling products online is a profitable and accessible alternative for entrepreneurs. You can sell

products online through a virtual store on sites like Shopify, Etsy, Amazon, or eBay.

3. Pet care services: Pet care services are an excellent option for animal lovers. You can offer services such as dog walking, in-home pet care, or pet training services.
4. Catering services: If you are passionate about cooking, you can offer catering services for events and parties. You can specialize in a specific type of cuisine or offer a variety of options.
5. Digital marketing consulting: If you have experience in digital marketing, you can offer consulting services to help businesses improve their online presence. You can help companies design digital marketing strategies, manage their social media, and improve their search engine rankings.
6. Gardening services: If you enjoy working outdoors, gardening services may be an excellent option for you. You can offer services such as garden maintenance, landscape design, installation of irrigation systems, among others.
7. Artisanal product store: If you are a craftsman or artist, you can open an artisanal product store to sell your creations. You can specialize in a specific type of product, such as jewelry, ceramics, or textiles.
8. Graphic design services: If you have skills in graphic design, you can offer design services for companies and individuals. You can design logos, brochures, posters, among others.
9. Personal training services: If you are passionate about fitness, you can offer personalized training services. You can train your clients at a gym, their home, or an outdoor space.
10. Virtual assistance services: Virtual assistance services are an excellent option for those looking to work from home. You

can offer services such as social media management, technical support, email management, among others.

Tips on credit that can help you improve your credit:

1. Know your credit score: It's important to know your credit score so you can take steps to improve it. You can obtain a free copy of your credit report annually from credit reporting agencies like Equifax, Experian, or TransUnion.
2. Pay your bills on time: A history of late payments can negatively affect your credit score. Make sure to pay your bills on time to avoid delays and additional charges.
3. Keep your credit card balance low: Keeping your credit card balance low can improve your credit score. Ideally, you should keep your credit card balance below 30% of your credit limit.
4. Don't close credit cards: Closing credit cards can negatively affect your credit score by reducing your total credit limit. Instead of closing them, try to keep them open and active to improve your credit history.
5. Use your credit cards responsibly: Use your credit cards responsibly to improve your credit history. Avoid spending more than you can afford and make sure to pay your bills on time.
6. Limit the number of credit cards: Having too many credit cards can be difficult to manage and can lead to excessive spending. Limit the number of credit cards you have to only those you need.
7. Regularly monitor your credit score: Regularly monitor your credit score to ensure you are taking steps to improve it. Use online tools like Credit Karma or Experian to monitor your credit score for free.

Here are some final tips based on the book:

1. Set clear and specific financial goals and work on them consistently.
2. Prioritize your debts and work on a plan to pay them off.
3. Learn to manage your money effectively and avoid unnecessary expenses.
4. Maintain a good credit score and regularly monitor your credit report.
5. Identify your personal skills and strengths and look for job or business opportunities that fit them.
6. Develop a positive and proactive attitude towards adversity and learn from your mistakes and failures.
7. Save for emergencies and plan for the future by investing in options that fit your financial goals.
8. Seek inspiration and advice from successful people and learn from their experience.
9. Maintain a consistent focus on your long-term goals and celebrate your achievements along the way.
10. Remember that resilience and perseverance are key to overcoming financial difficulties and achieving success.

The author suggests that financial success should not be limited to wealth accumulation and material possessions. Instead, it should be viewed as the result of continuous and persistent effort by an individual, regardless of their limitations or flaws.

This broader approach suggests that anyone can achieve financial stability through dedication, hard work, and perseverance, and that success is not limited to those who have economic or social advantages.

In summary, financial success depends not only on how much money one has, but on their ability to effectively manage their resources and work towards realistic and achievable financial goals. A successful career or book is not just about having all the money and fame, but rather about perseverance, resilience, and the ability to overcome obstacles despite adversity.

It's important to remember that even successful people have personal struggles and flaws, but what sets them apart is their ability to face and overcome those challenges.

In the end, it's about believing in oneself and having the discipline and determination to keep moving forward towards our goals, even when the road seems difficult.

"Overcome your fears, take control of your finances, and achieve financial success."

Made in the USA
Monee, IL
05 November 2026

67378292R00069